Peter Knaggs
You're so vain
you probably think this book is about you

You're so vain

you probably think this book is about you

Peter Knaggs

All rights reserved. No part of this book may be reproduced, stored in a retrieval system or transmitted in any form or by any means electronic, mechanical, photocopying, recording or otherwise, without the prior permission of the publisher.

ISBN 9781903110348

First published in this edition 2015 by Wrecking Ball Press.

Copyright Peter Knaggs

Cover design by Owen Benwell

All rights reserved.

ACKNOWLEDGEMENTS

The author would like to thank Gaia Holmes, Peter Sansom and Janet Fisher, Liz Barrett, The Bird Brothers and all the editors of the various fine magazines and journals, you deserve a bunch of flowers and/or a pint for publishing my poems in, Blah Blah Blah, Blurt, The Clockwork Fanny, The Ensign, Gumption, Hanging Jonny, Hubris, The North, Over Prudent Dog, Poetry Last Thursday, The Reater, Rue Bella, The Runcible Spoon and Containing Previously Unpublished Material; plus Hull City Council Transport Department for displaying "In That Direction" on a Princes Avenue bus stop. Much gratitude too to Dathidh MacEochaidh, the Skrev Press hero behind "Shakespeare Ate My Sonnet," in which a selection of these poems first appeared.

I would further like to thank the organisers and judges of The National Poetry Competition, The Bridport International, The Yorkshire Open, Hull Literature Festival, The East Riding, New Forest and BBC Wildlife magazine poetry competitions who awarded prizes to some of the poems herein. I would especially like to thank Nell Farrell, Dai Parsons, Dean Wilson and again Dathidh MacEochaidh. Your commitment to this poetry malarkey encourages and sustains me more than any of you can know.

CONTENTS

Staying Alive 9
Not Doing Owt 10
Industrial Relations 11
Her Brothers 12
Your Receipt's In Your Bag 13
The Doctors 14
The Man Who Ate Raven Soup (For Martin Mooney) 15
The Green Tree Lighting Company 16
I Knew God And The Devil (After Patrick Kavanagh) 18
Carrier Bags 19
Keeping The Shareholders Happy 20
On Customer Service 21
Crusoe's Mice 22
Two Losing Lottery Tickets In Her Purse 23
Bisto 24
Roofs 25
Crusoe's Prank 26
Crusoe's Love Song 27
For The Mermaid At Home 28
Me And The Mermaid 30
No Swimming 32
The Man Who Sits On Roofs 34
The Trapeze Artist's Grand Finale 35
Banana Dave's Halifax Adventure 36
Pyro 37
Skin And Bone 38
Shhhh 40
Warning, Cliché Hating Pikes Inhabit These Waters 42
Art For Fuck's Sake 43
Bring Me An Iron Lung 44
Car Boot Sale 45
Needless To Say I Didn't Have An Aquarium 46
If The Area Manager Had To Work Just One Day In A Goods In Area

They Might Never Park Their Expensive Car In A Loading Bay Again 47
Bruce Springsteen Is Good Music To Cook Risotto To 48
The Scam 49
Crusoe Buys A Book 50
Hell Hath No Fury 51
The Angler 52
The Poem Dave 53
Doing The Dog 54
The One Minute Manager Meets The Monkey 56
If My Careers Officer Could See My Now 57
Danny McGrain Never Played For Derby County 58
Ron Used To Have Just Two Tapes In The Cab 60
I'm In The Library 61
Play The Guitar 62
Today At Work I Put Out, To Sell, Fluffy Teddy Bear Bookmarks
With Santa Claus Hats. It's October 10th 63
Quartz On The Track 64
Poppy Tin Thief: "I'm So Sorry" 65
Wigginton Has A Donkey Called Primus
And A Hip Flask As His Companions 66
Airways, Breathing, Circulation 68
Fink 69
Badger The Cadger 70
Scunthorpe Police Swoop On Lunatic Bean Fetish Man 72
Half An Igloo 74
The Breakers 76
Hull 77
Slubberdegullion 78
Funny Bone 79
The Boisterous Shirt 80
In That Direction 81

STAYING ALIVE

Whenever he wanted anything he stole it,
like banana seeds from the garden centre,
C.B. radios from the local scout hut,
bottles of lager from the shop on the corner,

money from our changing rooms during P.E.
He chored pint glasses from the *Golden Lion*,
trousers and shirts from *Top Man* and *Burton*
did a runner from *The Taj* without paying.

His mother inherited a small fortune,
so she treated him to a 250cc motorbike;
he thrashed the arse off it - no insurance -
often crashed it, but never got killed.

NOT DOING OWT

We sit for lunch on cardboard boxes
waiting for the delivery, for lampshades
from Taiwan. Bobby puts a tape on.
We think he's robbed it from a car
because it's a compilation tape, right.
As if that's his writing, as if he could
write that neat, as if he would bother
making a tape, writing out the tracks,
numbering them, as if he could edit it
that precisely. *Did it last night*, he said.
As if. He's not called Bobby really,
it's just his nickname. He hates Billy.
Billy is eating a sandwich, white bread,
cut triangular, and when he puts it down,
it's impressed with grey fingerprints
like dabs down the nick. We ask
Bobby who the singers and bands
are on his tape and he doesn't know
any of them. Not even one.

INDUSTRIAL RELATIONS

Billy's mum makes his lunch every day.
His laugh annoys the fuck out of you,
grinds you down like the urrrr of the teeth
of this saw urrrrring in half these futon struts,
and Stepladder isn't overloaded in the brains
department, shakes his fingers and screams
BASTARD when he scalds them
with boiling glue and he's clumsy as chuff
so he sears his skin all day and he points
a ketchuped chip at me, eating with his gob full.
All he chunters on about all lunch time is
what a cunt Billy is and last night it snowed.
This morning Billy was pegging snowballs,
one whistled a mile by Stepladder's ear,
but that was enough. They were still rolling
around in the snow in the car park
when the gaffer opened up to let us in.

HER BROTHERS

Crusoe's up at five, out the house,
doesn't notice the black chimneys
stamp their shape against a lavender sky,
Crusoe's down the car wash whistling,
"Sweet Child O Mine." His van easily
the cleanest at *McCauleys Fruit & Veg*,
washed, meticulously, every day for the past
7 years. Crusoe has 3 different rags;
1 for the bodywork, 1 for the wheel arches
and a chamois for finishing off.
It gives him something to do
before leafing through the *Mirror*,
then the drive over to Leeds,
leaving his stumpy wife in bed.

At the start, he tried leaving a few times.
She'd show up at all hours, bawling foul-mouthed
accusations from her energetic gob, words twatting
him like the screech of worn down brake pads.
In the end he got scared of her brothers.
You daitless fuck-wit she calls him
or useless wank-stain, and other names.

YOUR RECEIPT'S IN YOUR BAG

Crusoe and her, they're used to each other
which counts for something like comfort;
and they understand that at Christmas,
she doesn't have to like the red lingerie
and he doesn't have to like that jumper,
so the receipts in the bag. Crusoe wonders
about people, people who live to shop.
He drops the van into second and aches to be
transported out of this mortgage-trapped slog.
Sometimes he wants God to give him
his receipt so he can take his whole life
back and get a refund; and sometimes,
if they're okay, he keeps her jumpers.

THE DOCTORS

When they sliced him in half
like a length of French loaf
they found he was all white and gold
like the white of the coat of an egg
and the sunshine of its yolk,
which he would have liked, seeing
as he was Leeds United through
and through, to the pip of the core
of his English apple, to the marrow
of his bone. And the cream of
his blood ran onto their aprons,
poured like Yorkshire pudding batter,
which would have pleased him
even more, him being Yorkshire,
from the northernest summit of his
shaven scalp to the southernmost tip,
flagging the nail of his biggest toe.
But he wouldn't have been chuffed
about them slicing him in half,
least of all before the ref blew,
with half a pair of bust scissors
and the arse-end of a table-spoon.

THE MAN WHO ATE RAVEN SOUP
FOR MARTIN MOONEY

He loved a bit of Raven soup
better than a breast of rook in his broth,
or lithe crow wing, or if forced to it,
starling, but he'd have to be starving.
Raven, it was like eating darkness,
drinking the inky essence of its soul.
The brute black beak and the feet
and the wet black eye in the pot
persuaded around the bubbling stock,
hunting him out, infecting him with
the royal raven swagger, their command
over their tarmac, him lording it over
his caravan. The fleshy purse of the carcass
is near enough cooked, he swabs
a blob of blood off the chopping board
with his thumb, sucks it and squawks.
He flexes the muscle of his wings, flaps.
He cuts three pieces of medium sliced
white bread in half, down the middle.

THE GREEN TREE LIGHTING COMPANY

It stopped with a fire extinguisher,
an ambulance butting into a punch up,
four staff dismissed for gross misconduct.
Ox started it, two inches of water

swill in a plastic coffee machine cup
couched between the door and its lintel,
leaning into the frame, precariously tilted,
a Laurel and Hardy slapstick ambush

and Billy exiting the crapper swearing
his head off at Ox. We'd be laughing
our cocks off, us. A cup of cold water
became a bog roll, a card box, a bucket,

once, a kettle. Until you couldn't
go for a slash without various bits
of workshop paraphernalia greeting
you with a Glasgow kiss. It starts

out, I would say, like this, horseplay,
a lark, call it Tomfoolery, but some people
can't take a joke, and other people take
a prank too far, like Ox, the prat.

And the gap between an inch or two
of tap water sitting in a beaker
and a not very funny fire extinguisher,
to be honest, is about the same

as the difference between getting the gag
and responding by kicking the joker
in the bollocks; or working the 100th
screw into the base of another bedside lamp

and sitting in *The Three Legged Maggot*,
a P45 stuffed in your back-pocket.

I KNEW GOD AND THE DEVIL
AFTER PATRICK KAVANAGH

I met them both at a board meeting.
The devil plugged in his laptop,
yattered about paradigm shifts
and improving customer interface.
He smiled. He was eager to get
us to understand how it was
all about K.P.I.s & R.O.C.E.
He wanted to run a campaign
promoting brand loyalty.
He was worried about the fickleness
of the general public, he ranted
about costs and turnover we were
running way above the industry
average. He wanted to know why.
Why were we losing so many staff?

God suggested compassion,
to give our people more money,
training, invest in long term growth,
the devil's sidekick butted in.
He had a plan, suspend the bonus,
make it quarterly, if staff leave
before the end of the quarter
they lose their bonus. God said,
'But,' but the devils were winning.

CARRIER BAGS

Next on the agenda, the implementation of savings.
A bloke at head office has calculated that if
we give every customer the smallest possible
carrier bag the reduction in expenditure would
be significant, a small bag costing 1.3p
and a large bag 2.5p. This idea could save
the company thousands. So H.O. have e-mailed
a memo to all branches - and any member of staff
caught thinking that head office people
are a bunch of twats, will not only be severely
reprimanded, but it could hamper their progress
through the career development framework.

KEEPING THE SHAREHOLDERS HAPPY

I am waving cheerio at the garden gate, going
to win some bread, saying tara to my wife
and girl whose one and three months and twenty
four days, tomorrow one and three months
and twenty five days, another day without her dad,
whose take home pay is less than enough over
the year to buy a small car; her dad whose money
goes on food, gas, electricity, water, T.V. license,
council tax, and near a fifth of his work time -
one day a week, is spent lining the pockets
of perk laden civil servants and politicians,
while the super rich pay accountants to concoct
schemes so that we, the underpaid, pay them.

It's no wonder I only get one fatigue-ridden day
with my wife and daughter, and the shareholders
who control my life, what do they know about all this?

ON CUSTOMER SERVICE

On the agenda, the falling standards
of customer service, the loss
of market share and the proportionate
loss in growth of future earning potential.

God spoke up, queried, "How can we have
long term growth while cutting back
on staff levels? We need good staff,
trained well, who spend time
with customers," The accountant
sitting on the right of the devil
is closely examining the office blind,
he says the company spends too much
on postage, they must stop sending
letters to customers, give them a couple
of weeks to collect their product, that
should save money on postage, yes.

CRUSOE'S MICE

They've been chewing the soap
in the soap dish by the basin
in the bathroom and leaving
traces in other places,

like footprints starring the fat
in the frying pan, a nocturnal
trot and they've shat behind
the spaghetti jar and Crusoe

wants to puke when he thinks
about shaking out their turds
from his toaster and those little
black smiles in the crunchy-

nut cornflakes. They crapped
in his grill-pan. It might
have been there a fortnight
camouflaged among the crumbs

and crispy blobs left from his
cheese on toast. Now Crusoe's
setting the traps, sliding the pin
into the node, it narks him

each time they snap back.
paggering his fingers, bastards.

TWO LOSING LOTTERY TICKETS IN HER PURSE

She died in a house full of plant pots,
with three cigarettes left in a packet,
two letters to post behind the mantel piece clock,
a dress, four blouses, two skirts in the wash,

an inch of milk past its date of expiry,
a saturated teabag in the bath of the teapot,
a coterie of bread crumbs specking the dish cloth,
somebody's black and white wedding photograph,

a bundle of leaflets and letters, the doormat.
All of these things were bunged into bin bags
to be chucked out, apart from the clock.
Her whole life was a slow puncture Bob

that never saw her inner-tube dunked
in a washing up bowl, the hole to fart bubbles
up the water, prescribing a puncture repair kit,
and they argued over her Spode and bracelets.

BISTO

On the news, the police
have the house surrounded,
the street cordoned off.
They're using a loud hailer.

A youth is holding his parents
hostage. They are in their
bedroom. The youth is known
to possess a fire arm.

It is unknown whether
the youth has any bullets.
The washing line is chafing
his daddy's wrists.

Marksman. Careful
were you lay your cross.
It's only McGuiffog.
He was OK at five a side.

I wouldn't say he was
the type of person whose
face muscles would be taxed
at the thought of a smirk.

You know, sometimes
he used to be in my class.

ROOFS

I'm the man that sits on roofs.
It's the quietness, the otherness,
the being above. I sit on roofs
most-times at night and doff out cigs
on the soles of my plimmys. Some nights
I'm soaked like a wet bird in the rain,
a drainpipe Tarzan, always careful.
Once, up a church, the pipe had rusted,
uncoupled itself, and I cartoon swung
a good hundred odd foot, up in the air,
I budged down sharpish like,
felt bad for knackering that pipe.

It's my birthday today,
so I'm over the wall at the stadium
and wiping the oil filming the glass face
of the floodlight. I love it up here,
just me and the floodlights
under the porcelain plate of the moon.
I love to hear the clunk of each metal step
run into the dark, watch below
an Alsatian bend its head one way,
being tugged by a security guard the other.

CRUSOE'S PRANK

We couldn't stop, not
once we had the idea
to bounce her car out
of its parking spot
and into the centre
of the street, to block
all the traffic. Laugh?
We laughed till tears
fell off our faces, we
couldn't stop. How were
we to know the handbrake
would snap & her mini
would roll, & we would
not be able to stop it
rolling downhill towards
& into the river Ouse.
It wouldn't stop, like
a *Malteser* dropped
onto a dining table.

CRUSOE'S LOVE SONG

Because I have paced this broken nose
of a street in this 500 strong insurance
clerk town and thought about my van,
or chucking it all in, to sell brochures
for the Viking Centre to Japanese tourists,
I have an excuse for dropping my trousers
outside MacDonald's and showing the staff
my arse.

FOR THE MERMAID AT HOME

Seagulls scratch their harsh names
on the sky with their raw voices.
I'm bashing limpets off the rocks
with my heel, creeping up on them
and chucking them into my pail
pressing its handle into the bend
in the bones in my fingers.

You laid out, at home in the bath
pushing house dust out of your nails
with a razor shell, missing mostly
this aroma, that I harvest
limpets to seaside the bath side,
wendletraps, sting winkles, scallops,
dog whelks, horse mussels, cowries,
cockles, fronds of seaweed, scurrying
hermit crabs, fossil-playthings.

I'm balancing by the rock pools
searching for the moons of Jupiter,
Io, Europa, Ganymede, Callisto,
but I have only my retina, iris,
pupil to search them out and I
can.

I can track sea creatures small
as a mustard seed with my
Hubble telescope eyes. At the pool
bottom, the corona of the sun
spreads itself like mustard.
I'm waggling my fingers looking
into infinity, to you mermaid
slouched in the bath, slopping
your comfortable tail, taking
a sea urchin tooth pick, picking
out crab meat, gazing at the grace
of the seahorses.

Me, I jump into the soft bounce
of the mattress of the seaweed and land.

ME AND THE MERMAID

Playing the hair-dryer again and again
through your hair while watching
your reflection in a pearl-studded
looking glass, eeny meeny miny mo-ing,
yes-ing, no-ing over shampoo for normal hair
and which conditioner? And now I'm wheeling
you out of *Superdrug* in your wheelchair,
a blanket draped to hide your tail.

The age it took to persuade you
to stick on a top, a coat or a cardigan.
On one hand you love so much to skate
your armpits with an electric razor.
But teeth? Now that's a totally different
kettle of crabs, toothbrushes and toothpaste
seem too peculiar a palaver, on the other hand
there's this delight at the ping of the microwave,
yet a deep-seated hatred of the electric kettle.
Me and the mermaid.

Your diet, cod, haddock, tuna, pilchards,
sild, sardines, herring, hake, squid, crab, prawns,
mussels, whelks, penny winkles; no chips,
batter or calamari, no sweet and sour sauce,
tomato ketchup, tartar sauce, salt or vinegar,
scampi or any other sea-fare product coated
in bread crumbs. You turn your perfect nose
up at kippers, bloaters, tuna in tins.
Raw fish only, the sound of it, your teeth
working the flesh off the spine, gnawing it
down to its bones, tail and fins, it stays
on your fingers that smell of the coast,
your mermaid skin holding the perfume
of the sea, me getting attached to things
like trawling up out of the plughole lengths
of your hair and picking off the wall
of the bath your marvellously iridescent scales,
much bigger than those of any fish
I've seen before in my life. Even carp.

NO SWIMMING

We've stolen out to the marina,
a space age shopping centre
on aluminium stilts in a Victorian
harbour. You are almost singing,
tucking the song under your tongue,
releasing it out of captivity into
the wild city, under the hub cap
of the moon. Shop light is
gilding my hair, silvered by the soup
of the water, soothed by the balm
of the night. The ripples from the slap
of your tail submerging, retract
to a bellybutton of water.
It bursts the tranquil surface
your mermaid head. Behind me
is a city closed down, Burton's
on the corner 20% off all footwear.
My bare feet tread water, treading
a nebulous platform of sea, so
liberating a midnight dip in the
centre of the city. You swimming
towards me, arms blue like a car
in an advertisement. On the day
God made animals he must have made
mermaids. How? Did he sculpt or mould

like a potter on God's potters wheel,
or was it more like an *Airfix* kit,
the assembling of us, the spitting
on the hands of it? Mad for it,
mashed in the teapot of it,
deliciously demented and alive.
No Swimming

I'll step out soon, leaving nothing
but the clouds of my breath, taking
only drops of the sea beaded
to my body, I'll shake it out of my hair
like a dog, then watch you like the sailor
in the crows nest peeling his eyes
for the harbour. There are only us two,
me pressed cold to the stone, you
mermaid girl, swimming this way,
gripping a fresh sprat in your teeth.

THE MAN WHO SITS ON ROOFS

It's me again, up here in black plimsolls
and fierce blue mohair sweater, listening
for the chicaning of water around the basin,
the clunk of the chip tray buckling in the oven,
the T.V. host goading the quiz contestant,
the groan of the kettle coming to the boil,
the squeak against drainpipe of black plimsoll,
the bite of the night of an Italian flick knife,
the recoil of it sitting back on its spring,
the dulcet lost song of a landlubbered pirate,
the passing over tonight, of the black spot,
the shock inhale of blind superstition,
the warble of my own voice in a younger skin
praying to God while rubbing like worry beads
a Saint Christopher in the form of a silver coin,
as if being embossed with an image of Christ,
banks in it the soul and ear of Our Lord.
"Please God, please God, don't let it happen."
"Please God, please God, make it happen."
"I promise not to ask for anything else."

THE TRAPEZE ARTIST'S GRAND FINALE

To the hushed crowd he salutes, half man half sequin,
at the top of the big top, in the spotlight, he glistens.
The coxcombries of the bigfooted clowns get a laugh
as they buffoon away the safety net. The ringmaster hushes
down the crowd. This death defying feat needs absolute silence,
not a whisper, not the tiniest mush of popcorn versus tooth,
a scratch of the lobe, a sharp intake of breath. Please ladies
and gentlemen be nailed, still, to that moment, the moment
he swings with ballet grace. Right now, a slip the distance
of a span of the hand, or a grasp missed of the time it takes
for the palms to make a single clap, would prove fatal.

In that dive forward, I want to swim through the air,
to catch those acrobat hands. Right then, I could still love him.
But in this game, it's all about trust. The idea of him prowls
the confines of my brain, a vision of him exiting her porch.
He must concentrate now. The circus-time crowd
tip their chins right up, he swoops forward
the two-timing twat! I cough. The audience
bring their chins down to their chests, and gasp.

BANANA DAVE'S HALIFAX ADVENTURE

The slops of a coffee sit in a cup.
The cigarette has burnt right down to its stump.

Two models perform a perfunctory hug
on a poster selling *Fruit of the Loom* stuff.

Fruitknife stores the breath for a flute.
Banana fingers the collar of his suit,

he'd love a saxophone but can't play
a note. Fruitknife coughs to clear his throat.

The floorboards thump to a child's steps.
Coffee and cigarette on his breath,

he pulls out of his pocket a roll of notes,
waves them under the shopkeeper's nose.

PYRO

I wish I was out in the wood with the boys,
drinking meths, watching the birch logs curl back
their bark in the heat, or spreading out my fingers
to warm them against a burning car tyre;
us cauling our windpipes on rhododendron cigarettes,
maybe Woodsy doing his tricks, spitting meths
into the fire and the fire whooshing up
that lavender colour; or swimming a blazing blob
in his palm, a tiny puddle of amazing blue,
or later waving his hand through the camp-fire
flames as, *"They're not so hot,"* us squinting
our eyes at the hilarity of it all, swigging back
tins of it and Woodsy's cagoule on fire
all the way up his arm. All of us, the next day,
singed across the eyebrows, dirt in our nails,
dirt on our faces, smelling like kippers.

SKIN AND BONE

Me sixteen; me all skin, all oxblood monkey boots,
laces bright as buttercups; all pop music T shirts,
Madness and Tracey Ullman on the radio the whole
summer long; me all bone. Me, all on a placement
on the Youth Training Scheme, on the eighth floor
of *Smarties* packing; me, all the smell of the cocoa.
Me remember smell of firelighters in the massive lifts
with those weighty criss-cross trellised gates.
Me first day, all skin, pockets crammed with fistfuls
of *Smarties* in the cubicle in the toilet. Me all white
hygiene hat, elastic rim impressing into my skull,
me clocking off, chucking it in my locker, it feeling
as though I'm still wearing it, all tea break, pint mugs,
back to it with that big numb old bastard, who never
wore socks or laces in his boots, who nearly got fired
for crouching down in front of a visiting group,
and letting his bollocks fall out of the hole in the crotch
of his kecks. Me all bone in a department full of women,
thinking it funny too, when asked me sixteen,
if I was a virgin, cheeks furnacing me giving my monkey
boots a good inspection. Me trained box *Smarties*,
in that glasshouse. *Smarties* are dull at first,
when they're painted. They gain that crayon gloss
when coated with wax, bright like the sheen
on the lithe thighs of those twenty-summat factory girls.
It was so hot, they'd just strip to knickers and bras
beneath their white dust coats. They'd cross their
tantalising legs on their high stools and didn't mind me,
or forgot about me. Me sixteen, un-noticed, unseen.

They had *Smarties* to box, work to do, they'd lean forward,
sideways, lift and drop, their press studs would un-pop,
I'd see flashes of tummy buttons, catch glimpses of bra straps,
sometimes that illicit soft part at the top of the breast,
as they'd stretch or maybe bend, and those legs. Me; I'd see
so high up, it would scare the Bejasus out of me; sixteen, all skin,
all monkey boots, all bone. More than anything I ached
to look. Nothing could urge me to. But my inadvertent
eyes would face that way... sometimes... just then.

SHHHH

My predicament is this.
I have the bottle in my hand;
don't want to have the bottle
in my hand, to pace that way,
towards the restless noise.
But it's my job to pace
towards the noise tonight
to find out what is going on
and if I need the bottle.

My predicament is this.
I have the bottle in my hand;
my hand is fourteen years old
and my fingers may have to
pincer the limp pork sausage
of his penis and plop it into
the neck of the bottle so a jet
of piss can stream inside.

My predicament is; I want
to run. I want to run all the way
home and forget the noise
that may or may not be
a 21 year old man wanting
a piss and me never having
touched another man's cock.

My predicament is this;
I've done the corridor,
now I'm here, by the bed,
I've sourced the noise, and
Paul is thrashing on his bed
like a landed pike. I have
the bottle in my hand.

He understands when I ask
if he needs a slash; and I
understand he's being kept
awake by something altogether
different. His huge erection
waggling about says it's not his
bladder that needs to be emptied.

WARNING, CLICHE HATING PIKES INHABIT THESE WATERS

It was devastating to open the fridge
and the fridge to have no milk whatsoever
for cornflakes - gutted - or worse, tea -
double gutted. So, I were sat sagging
in my chair, the postman sidled past
our house, no letters. I was so gutted.
Then it started raining. Man I was gutted,
absolutely gutted. Anyhow Cowboy Hat
came round, so I stuck me fishing gear
in his boot. All the way he played this
tape of Marillion. I was really gutted
about that. We found our spot by the river.
Cowboy Hat caught the first fish.
I was absolutely gutted. Then my waggler
started bobbing, I struck and reeled
in this fish, it was big and nasty, it had
a Bowie knife in its fin. It sliced
my tummy and pulled my entrails out.

ART FOR FUCK'S SAKE

Chewing the fat with Crusoe.
Art! He knows what it is
and it isn't a nude woman
stood in the arcade on a soap box
with a tumbler and a jug
of water, drinking the water
and waiting and drinking,
waiting until she pisses herself.
Crusoe admits though that it does
provoke an emotional response.
People like that,
he wants to kick their fuckin heads in.

BRING ME AN IRON LUNG

Bronski Beat were always on the radio,
'Hit that perfect beat boy, beat boy,'
which we changed to, *'Big boys, big boys,*
Malcolm's into big boys.' Even now,
when I hear that song, the lyrics have been
permanently converted. It gets me thinking
about Malcolm. We were bad, constantly
picking on him.

                    You know that plastic
strapping you get on bundles of newspapers?
Well; we used to have a machine that did that
strapping, for our lights and lampshades,
the bander, it heated up the end of the strapping,
tightened the bundle, melded the two ends
together. Once, right, we put Mal, that's what
we called him, Mal, in this box and banded it up.
We put about thirty bands on this box
and lobbed it into the skip. A fist jostled
it's way out of one corner, his tramps shoe
kicked out the opposite corner. Hot Chocolate
were in the charts. It made us laugh, we were
sure he was singing, *'I believe in Malcolm*
where you from... you sexy thing.'
Go on, have a listen. I don't know why
I mentioned that Bronski Beat thing.

CAR BOOT SALE

Crusoes fossicking through a cutlery draw
of chafed spoons and scuffed forks.
There's a mended telly and a *Trangia*.
Crusoe spots a Victorian photo
in a simple frame. The thick glass is so good.
It has a home-made charm. Crusoe asks,
how much? He'd go to a couple of quid.
The stallholder wants 20p. Crusoe gives him it.

In his house, Crusoe studies this indistinct photo
of a boy, about 8 years old.
It's ungraspable to him that anyone would
keep this haunting picture. It must mean
something. Why would anyone go to the trouble
of building the frame, fixing on the glass
and the chain and hang it on the wall,
this photo of a boy, with his head chopped off?

NEEDLESS TO SAY I DIDN'T HAVE AN AQUARIUM

You'd steal. I've done it, as a perk of the job or something
you just do, particularly when it's hard to make ends meet.
you, unloading by hand whole containers full of boxes
of lampshades, 25 kilos a box, hundreds of boxes.
So, accidentally on purpose, say there's a delivery
for someone else on the same wagon, Bobby would
divert a couple into the unpacking room, empty out
the contents, tape the boxes back up, come out, grinning,
sorry mate, these two aren't ours, hand them back
to the driver. We'd divvy up the booty.
I got six tea spoons with teddy bear handles, two clocks
made like an owl, the clock-face on his tummy, a dozen
aquarium fish nets and twenty three aquarium pumps.

IF THE AREA MANAGER HAD TO WORK JUST ONE DAY IN A GOODS IN AREA THEY MIGHT NEVER PARK THEIR EXPENSIVE CAR IN A LOADING BAY AGAIN

On a different matter, our area manger is visiting
our store tomorrow. He wants to see how efficient
we are and to berate us for any slackness in our
standards of customer service. I've got forty five
customers whose orders haven't arrived yet,
whose lampshades need chasing up, but no.
I dust all day long, to make the shop look tidy
for our area manager. No one tells him, hey
*we've got nearly fifty customers screaming
for their lampshades,* and I'm sure if we told them,
*your order hasn't arrived yet, but hey, our shelves
are lovely and shiny,* they wouldn't be impressed.

BRUCE SPRINGSTEEN IS GOOD MUSIC TO COOK RISOTTO TO

but the phone rings. It's Banana Dave.
Do I fancy a pint in five minutes?
Course I do. As I neck the first
of the night, the risotto is yet

to stop bubbling. Banana looks old.
His nose drops down like a courgette stub.
His nostrils are like fireplaces. Arsenal,
he thinks, will win the league. The charts are crap,

full of manufactured shite. His skin falls
into his gob like a shirt falling off
an ironing board. His cheeks are pushed in
like thumbed in milk bottle tops. Banana tells me

every thing's all right, every thing's OK. You know.
It takes him five pints to get round to it.
It's the house. He can't go back to the house,
it just feels so empty, now his mam's gone.

THE SCAM

Arnie trying to be as normal as can be
expected, Arnie practising his casual patter,
Arnie holding the words close to his chest,
thirty four thousand please, cool as you please,
Arnie with his muddy rucksack, acting
as if it is a normal activity, going into
a building society and asking calmly yet
politely for thirty four thousand in cash
please. Arnie hoping his voice doesn't go
all high at the counter, like it does now
and then. Arnie getting closer to the counter,
Arnie slipping his rucksack off of his shoulder.

CRUSOE BUYS A BOOK

to better his sen, it tells him,
'If you think you are happy, then you will be.'
His mum dies.
He still wants to improve his lot, so he buys
a different book. It tells him, *'The important*
thing is not to give up.' So he drives around
the industrial estates and dawdles around
the shopping arcades. He asks hundreds
of gormless schmucks for work, but,
despite his resourcefulness, energy, drive,
enthusiasm and ambition, no one offers him
a job. He reads chapter 2, it tells him to network.
His dad's on the dole. His mum's a cleaner,
so he uses social media to look up
his old classmates, he phones Stiggy,
they go for a pint. Stiggy left school,
bummed around, travelled a bit,
then his uncle gave him a job in marketing,
loads of money - car - Crusoe should try it.
Crusoe goes home. He reads the final chapter.
It says, *'Life is a mirror, sometimes you have to*
smile into it.' Crusoe thinks about Stiggy, about
all those temping agency staff Stiggy hasn't had to
butter up, all those regret to inform you letters
Stiggy hasn't had to read, how each one
subtracts something from you like an ice
cream man scooping the ice cream of life from his
ice cream tub of impassiveness.

Crusoe thinks about Stiggy and all that confidence.
Crusoe looks at himself
in his shabby bathroom mirror; doesn't smile.

HELL HATH NO FURY...

Gasher stuck a blade into Pigeon,
into the gut, into the heart.
It had been a good idea
of Gasher's to gag the lad,

aye, the brutal refusal to accept
being hacked in the chest.
Gasher's wife would now – not
find out. Yes, it was all over

at Pigeon's request. "Just once
more, mate." He'd made a pact,
yet even as Gasher despatched
the promise from his mouth

he'd tossed around the thought
of this empty house. He wipes
his spunk off, on Pigeon's shirt,
he won't mind much. The blade

mentioned earlier was the blade
of a pair of shears for the hedge,
so the neighbours would think
he'd come to snip some twigs.

Pigeons out of his final breath,
shears stuck like a scarecrow
into the field of his chest.
Gasher is at the all night garage

picking up a paper, a coke
and a packet of cigarettes.

THE ANGLER

When people ask me, in libraries how I got started in poetry
I tell them about that time I was fishing in the river Foss
and my coffin lead got tangled in the deadly nightshade,
so I stumble over, my 3lb *Bayer Perlon* line invisible,
the lob worm dug from our garden wriggling mid-air.
And I'm pulling my fishing line out. I see this bottle.
It's a wine bottle all waxed up at the top, it's muddy
and inside is a note. I take the bottle over to my rucksack
by my fishing gear and I take out my pen-knife and chip
at the wax. Inexpertly I de-cork it. The cork breaks
and I end up pushing the cork into the bottle
with a porcupine quill. I try for ages to pull up the paper.
The coil of paper has sprung, wider than the neck.
In the end, I do get it out. On the paper is a poem.
It's about this bloke in a factory. I like it. It's about
how tired you get, how the other people can be arse-holes.
I carry the bottle with me everywhere, in my coat pocket,
for the next ten years. Then one day I'm in the *Three
Legged Maggot* and an older Scottish man engages me
in conversation. Anyhow, he notices the bottle and asks
about it. So I tell him the story, of how I found the bottle
while fishing all those years ago. I tell him how I carry it
around with me and read the poem every now and then.
I've no idea of the author. The Scottish man takes a look
at it, reads it, and tells me it's an early poem by the great
Barnsley poet Geoff Hattersley. That's what I tell people,
when they ask me, in libraries, how I got started in poetry.

THE POEM DAVE

I raise money for charity. At least I did once,
years back, for a bus, to take special people
on day trips. I spent a whole night with my left leg
tied to Dave's right leg. We called him Animal.
Animal was a plumber. At dinner time sometimes
he'd stuff his moy with fish and chips, twice.
Once, he knocked his sen unconscious, in his
Romeo, by twatting his head against the window.
When he came round, he chuckled, muttered,
"I thought it was open." Animal and myself
were diligent, unlike others, about staying tied
together, it was an honesty thing. As if we'd betray
our generous sponsors by un-tethering our sens.
We pissed together. Or one of us would wait
while the other had a slash. Come to think of it,
Dave might have even had a shite, me waiting
on the other side of the cubicle door.
Our target was to drink half a pint in each of 20
pubs. We did it for charity, and people paid me
for drinking beer while tied to Animal Dave.
Forty two pounds I raised; most of my friends
on that three-legged pub crawl raised more
than me. They never bought a bus.
I don't know where the money went, okay!

DOING THE DOG

I thought I better tell you, arse hole, you can stick your job,
hour after hour paggering my knees, caking my fingernails
with dirt, to get pulled up by that clever fucker for the slightest
squint of muck, my thumbnail worn to a stub scratching up
splodges of three day old carbonara sauce or splodges
of whatever stuff it is that rich people eat. And that vacuum cleaner;
Bend over son, I'll ram it right up your jacksey if it breaks down
one more fucking time. I've had it up to here with all this,
Calm down, calm down. You, you smug bastard sitting pretty
in your Alpha Romeo, push button windows, Thelonius Monk
on the CD player, Terry Pratchett novel on the passenger seat,
squash racket in the boot. Me practising those high strokes
on fag smoke, Caramacking the emulsion, fugging up the gaps
in the sash windows, reaching out for high spots
like the pelmets and the long slim cranny of the cornice,
me pal, mopping the tide marks of the bath,
rendering their scum invisible. Those petty notes an' all,

'Do not dust the golden Buddha today or move the money
tree from it's optimum west corner Feng Shui position.
For the fig leaf tree use the blue J cloth in the orange tub
in the right hand corner of the cupboard under the sink.'

but what really gets me are those tiny little hairs, you know the ones
I mean, pubes. Do the rich grow more than the poor or what? I'm sick
of picking them up, seeing them stare at me from underneath
the toilet seat, nests of them. But it were her that got to me,
not him, him lurking all the time, hands on hips like a teapot.
He booked me because of our ad, *'Floors scrubbed in the old
fashioned manner, on hands and knees, by maids in traditional
uniform.'* Well you can swivel on this sunshine. Doggy fashion,
we all know that position. The position you want me in.
But I'll tell you something, I only get in the position for one person
and even for him, not that often.

THE *ONE MINUTE MANAGER* MEETS THE MONKEY

Our manager tells us that we should see our jobs,
our tasks, as monkeys. That some monkeys are ours
and some are other peoples, he says we should feed
them and make sure they get enough shelter and sleep.
He doesn't mention dustpans brooms, monkey baba.
Out of the staff meeting and down the stairs,
in the shop, the phones ring their heads off,
at the till points, monkeys wait with enquiries.
These are not my monkeys. It's my job to sort
out all the monkey orders, their letters, e-mails,
the discrepancies in their invoices, their delivery
notes and deposits. The gibbons are thumping
the back door bell with deliveries,
there are eight or nine trolleys of stock
to be shelved; more waiting to be sorted
and priced. In fact the delivery room is full
of everyone else's monkeys, mostly head office's
monkeys. I've never seen anyone from head office
come to our branch to sort their monkey out.
The orang-a-tangs with their baskets of shopping
are getting impatient, I grab the hectoring phone
and a chimpanzee goes oooh oooh oooh ahrr aaa
aaar ooo ooo aa ahhhr aaahr, aaahr aaahr aaahr.

IF MY CAREERS OFFICER COULD SEE ME NOW

I tell lies to taxi drivers. I don't know why!
They just enter my head and exit my moy.
As we coast to a junction, *I'm a wine-buyer
for Tesco, just last week I was in Bulgaria.
Next week I'm jetting off to the sun-drenched
hills of California. It's OK, but the long hours,
I miss my kids.* Or as he slips into second,
*I'm a scout for Bolton Wanderers, checking
out a nippy left back in Doncaster Rovers
youth team.* Sometimes, *I put the stripes
in toothpaste, down the factory,* or as I tell
him, *Left here mate. I'm in the final
design stages of the newest Mars Bar wrapper.*
Taxi drivers, I like them, even those
that don't say a word, despite the thought
that I can't imagine one ever boasting,
*Hey, do you know who I had in my cab?
That poet bloke, that geezer, what's-is-name?*
all the other cabbies looking up in wonder, *Never.*

DANNY MCGRAIN NEVER PLAYED FOR DERBY COUNTY

Douglas never got used to it,
kept on phoning us after it,
like we were still friends.
He'd joke about the jolts
of electricity burning his brain,
the colours of his pills,
the colour of his piss.
When in town, he's after
meeting up for cocktails
with us, all of us, even Dan,
like he never swished his chest
with a Stanley-knife. Douglas
gets boisterous on the phone
with Shirley when we don't show up.
It's like Douglas thinks we could
still carry on joking,
Douglas laughing in Scottish
about him opening, inadvertently,
mail to his landlady's partner,
it being an impotency clinic
test result. Ha ha. But we'd only be
laughing to keep him happy,
to keep him cheery Douglas from
Glasgow with his Glasgow twang,
not Douglas the sulky foul-tempered
orphan from Bolton, who could

spiral from the minor fact that
Danny McGrain never played
for Derby County, (he never did).
to that difficult management meeting,
which Douglas seems to have either
not comprehended, or completely deleted,
the one where he became re-acquainted
with his P45

for violent conduct.

RON USED TO HAVE JUST TWO TAPES IN THE CAB

Blondie, *Parallel Lines*, and *Showaddywaddy's
Greatest Hits*, but somehow it was all the music
Ron needed. That summer I'd watch them
climb into the cab and the way Ron danced
in his seat while driving, the way they said,
Come on Ron, get a tape on.
They'd sing, Lets Go For A Little Walk,
and drum on the dashboard, in time to the music,
click their fingers to, Run-a-round Sue.
Ron would nod his shaggy head of black hair,
Doo wah diddy, diddy dum diddy doo,
we'd bounce out of the cab to deliver a sofa
or a cupboard and we'd swagger, we'd swing,
we were rockers and rollers we were Showaddy Waddy,
we were Debbie Harry.

How many tapes does anyone need?

I often think of Ron and those two tapes,
the only tapes he played in the cab, for months,
possibly years. Maybe Ron knew something,
or knows something, that we don't.

I'M IN THE LIBRARY

I see

Injection Mould Design
A Design Manual For The
Thermoplastics Industry.

It has been in the library since 1985
and no one has ever borrowed it,
something about it reminds me of my manager.

PLAY THE GUITAR

And while I am at work, lifting,
loading, boxing, shelving,
it appears some people are not working,
some people talk a bit and laugh;
like this guy on the radio,
playing a few records, that's not work!

As for this woman he's interviewing,
a colour psychologist.

A colour psychologist?

Jesus!

Definitely not working. Helen's working,
even Dean's working, and I'm working
and listening to this highly paid joker
on the radio tell us that Manchester
is the place where people are
least likely to wear flip-flops,
for work, according to a survey.

TODAY AT WORK I PUT OUT, TO SELL, FLUFFY TEDDY BEAR BOOKMARKS WITH SANTA CLAUS HATS. IT'S OCTOBER 10TH

...and I am asked to turn out my pockets. In my right hand
I hold a light blue handkerchief and a bunch of keys,
in my left hand various bits of paper with phone numbers,
ISBNs and my shifts scribbled on, the normal stuff
for a person working in a bookshop. He says, disinterestedly,
'Is that all?'

And I wonder what he means. Can he not see the indignity
of one adult asking another to turn their pockets out?
An employee of fourteen years, trusted with a budget running
into tens of thousands of pounds, an honest person who puts
mutual trust at the very centre of their being, who feels so
violated and insulted by the very idea that he would dip his
fingers into the till for a few quid. Can he not see the bitter
resentment simmering right there on my fingers? The security
guard who calls himself a loss prevention officer, can he see it?

I don't think he can.

QUARTZ ON THE TRACK

It shines like the moon at the end of a tunnel.
Fruit Knife, let's chew the fat over this greatest ever
being drunk story. You say you were that blabbered

you keeled out on the railway track,
when the world coalesced, your leg was gone.
You haven't a clue what happened, in theory.

Funny though, that night, you'd split with your lover.
Others tell me you took a hand held pick axe down
to the track, to square things up with your Bête Noire,

to backstitch the quartz of the moon through
the tunnel. You could never exist without him.
He had severed his life from yours, but Fruit knife

you still felt it, the brain receiving messages from
the nerve-tips of the phantom limb, how kind of it to acquiesce
with your inkling, he's not gone. My theory is this.

Fruit knife, you got scared last second. Couldn't do it.
And like the sweep of a Heath Robinson lightsaber,
the train wheels coincided with your escaping leg.

POPPY TIN THIEF: "I'M SO SORRY"

A man who stole a poppy collection tin
on Remembrance Sunday has apologised
and said he feels like, "Scum."
The man took the tin from a Hessle Road shoe shop
just hours after the nation stood in silence
to remember the war dead. He said

I am stupid, I am scum. I can't believe I did it
I have been clean from drugs for three years
and I am even allowed to take my methadone
unsupervised because they trust me.
I used to steal things all the time
but I haven't been in trouble for two years.
There is nothing I can do to undo it.

The Hull man, it was heard in court,
has 29 previous convictions for shop theft
and was serving a two-year suspended sentence
for theft when he committed his latest offence.

I can't take it back, I can't wind back the clock,
I'm sorry for what I did.
I am sorry it ever crossed my mind.
He added, "I will give The Royal British Legion
fifty quid on Friday from my benefits
and I will give them fifty quid in a fortnight.
Hopefully that will go some way to show I'm sorry.
I am heartbroken. I cried during my interview;

I don't even know why I did it.
I had a hundred and fifty bar on me
from selling a dog.

WIGGINTON HAS A DONKEY CALLED PRIMUS AND A HIP FLASK AS HIS COMPANIONS

Primus points forwards, a weather vane
signalling the direction of the bitter rain.
The punishing clouds muster like oaty brose,
cumulus tempering the mash potato heels
of cumulonimbus, a cloud street engine lugs
his brothers and sisters to spit on the road.

Wigginton smitten, the hope he rode
that summer, love infiltrating his veins,
the throaty way she chuckled, *"buggerlugs,"*
always singing, *Dancing in the Rain.*
He felt better than ever before, not vain,
it's just that feeling inside him brews.

For the 3rd time Wigginton sips the athol-brose.
It's like a hub-cap careering down the road
escaping. Whisky. Ice. The drink heals
helps to lose a faculty, a function, a vain
hope to discolour the judgement, to hold back, rein
in and scramble and turn him all brain-slug.

Wigginton knots and ropes up the log
for Primus the donkey to tug, a hangover bruises
his brain. He remembers. He forgets, reins
and bridles Primus to take the chalky road.
Will he always have ice and whisky veins
and a pair of boots with clarted heels?

No redemption, just a living hell.
Remembers that night, pinches the lobe of his lug,
it's a compulsion when he's in that vein
of thought, the burden of regret festers, brews,
the twin tyre tracks slipping off the road.
The alcohol toxins are caught by the rane.

In the accommodation of the virulent rain
he lost control of the steering wheel.
She had died by the time the cockerel crowed.
Out of the muddy beck, the ambulance men lugged
the two, Wiggington barely a scratch or bruise.
They attempted to resuscitate in vain.

The benison rain smothers Primus and Wigginton lugpoint
to hoof tip, cleans and heals each life-long bruise
gained on the road, almost absolves the guilt in each vein.

AIRWAYS, BREATHING, CIRCULATION

...fuckin so hot, got cobwebs in my throat,
got to get back, got to get back, got to get
back with my stretcher, some fans, some
fans are unconscious on the pitch,

banging up against each other, pensioners,
hair growing out their ears, young lasses,
the lost chance of a kiss gracing their lips,
mostly inert, some twitch. Some fans mill

by the touchline. Kneel, bollocks, my black trousers
scuffed with penalty box pitch markings.
A-B-C, these three lads first, out cold, breathing.
It's a hasty, a flamingo-toed paddle back through

the arms and legs of fans. At the ambulance,
wrestle with my breath, hoist the stretcher up.
No time to waste, not enough of us, get back,
get back, got to get back, a prat of a cameraman

right up my arse. A ferocious urge to just twat
the bastard detonates inside me. Calm down.
A-B-C. Calm down. I've got to get back.
The sun is glazing the faces of them lads,

before this pall starts settling itself over us,
I've got to get back, got to stay professional.

FINK

Whassat, that muzzled rumble, its a hand in a kitchen drawer,
harassing a nest of tea towels and napkins and that solo decibel
grazing the base of my ear-lobe is a cupboard hinge opening out
to scouring pads, shoe polish, shoe brush, car wax.
That tap tap tapping like a twig against the brick, it's the riffling
through of the plastic sheaves of my compact discs, *Shoulders,
The Guillemots, Star Catcher, Gas Bag*, unsuitable swag.

Was that that gust smacking the gate shut or the dislocated chink
of a handful of our saucers being badgered into a sack?
Did you hear a clatter, then, like crows on the tiles infiltrating
my yawny brain? It was the plasticky shake of the electrical cord
of the toaster snaked up, handballed to a henchman with a holdall.

I'm dozy but that curt clitter scuffing the rim of my lug
could well be the final soup spoon being shepherded into
a shoplifter's pocket. And I would go back to sleep, but is that not
a spot of torch-light sailing the dresser crammed with glassware,
hunting out the prospect of silverware or jewellery, breaching
a private moment tethering itself to the wedding photo. Listen.

The pickings here are uneasy pie. Through the confines
of the wash-kitchen, ferret for a scrim to brighten the pawnbroker's eye,
find light-bulbs, shed paint, garden candles. Tottle out the cargo
of my toolbox, copper wire, six inch nails, 3 amp fuses, that's all.
Please go. Stop. I can hear the groan of you sifting through the shelf
of left-over gloss, the clap of your glove disguising your prints,
and that glassy bump is the distinct scud of *Doc Marten*,
against milk bottle, it drops and rolls forth and back on the path all night.

BADGER THE CADGER

He eats like a blithering slotterhodge
trowelling grub into his gob
at the mercurial speed of a wild hyena
or some other vulture-like prairie dog,

stuck in a dry and desolate place, no food
for days. The slobberchops tops his sen
up from the pit of his oversized slote
to the whistle-stop-hole of his gullet.

The slathertrash slammacks a course
through the restaurant like a drunken boat
in his button-shorn, spanwhengled coat,
camouflaging sauce spots, years old,

hair haystacked into the fashion of a fleabitten
hedgehog, pancaked to the road,
that could only be contrived by
a supreme fonkin with a toothless comb.

He's a salivary slathering slobberchops,
a porknell, a ructatious snuffling slopper,
supper lover, wheel-barrow-guts,
a gluttinous, guzzling, ill-mannered glopper.

Not a snattock of respect in appearance
or dress. A spaghetti splatt of slurpy mess
bolognesing one of his backswiped chins.
That sound of a plughole draining is him,

gurking, ramming pie down his thropple. Distant.
Engaged in another different day of this life,
on how when you topple you can drop like
a kite. Then in his own voice he asks for the bill,

pockets losing touch with their stitches,
full to the brim with sparrows tickets.

SCUNTHORPE POLICE SWOOP ON LUNATIC BEAN FETISH MAN

Back in Scunthorpe, police
confirmed they'd made an arrest in the baked beans
case. A Scunthorpe
man has been taken into custody. Mother
is interested in this incident.
I phone her right

away. "Mother can you hear me all right?
It's been on the telly, the police
have arrested some loony. Remember that incident,
that woman, barefoot, beans,
yeah, that's right mother,
they've got this fella in Scunthorpe,

in Waterstone's, in Scunthorpe,
he tried it again right,
told the girl to close her eyes, mother,
poured beans on her nude foot. She called the police.
The police kept some for evidence, the beans,
incidentally,

this is about the seventh time, seventh incident,
all young women, in Scunthorpe,
all shop assistants, each time beans.
They think he's doing it for Comic Relief, right,
so they pull their socks and shoes off, for a laugh. Police
have warned them, nowt to do with charity, mother,

he's a fraud, an impostor, a nut-job, mother,
seven incidents
in the last two weeks. The police
in Scunthorpe
became suspicious when, right,
he didn't ask for any cash. He's been

known to take a photo of the beansmothered
foot, mother.
These young lasses must be shaken. He sounds like a right
weirdo. It was on the news today, the latest incident.
It isn't safe to be a shop assistant in Scunthorpe.
Well it is now, now they've made an arrest. The police

have been after this beans man since that incident
in Mothercare, seven shops in Scunthorpe,
this beans nutter has hit, until now avoiding the police.

HALF AN IGLOO

Don't tickle it. Punch it laddie.
He shows me how to punch it.
Bastard. I pretend it's him,
my shirt cling-filmed to my back.
My wrists all kibed and chafed
by these red industrial gloves,
I pack and box the snow
into the wooden snow-brick mould.

I am occupied as a builder
of igloos. I have a schedule
as tight as a huskies snatch.
So I put my sweaty back into it.
I love it. It feels euphoric
raising the most fantastic
igloo you ever clapped eyes on.

Eskimo boss has stopped bawling.
His skidoo has droned
into the frail white distance.
He doesn't want problems.
He only wants answers.
His deadline allows
no consideration for penguins
under my iced wet socks
and this polar bear is really
starting to gnaw my nipples.

For every snow-brick square I set,
while I crouch to the spirit-level,
he sets too with his smudge of nose.
Each brick I lay, nudges one free
in a nonchalant game. They splatter
and break. I might laugh, kersplat,
ramshackle penguins under my boots,
but it's not his pay getting docked,
not his paws chilblaining up.
And the snow smoothing my collar
melts against the nape of my neck
and it melts in the steam of my breath
and it melts in the cloud of his breath
but it takes to his fur and spreads.

THE BREAKERS

Hull City Council promised they would pick up the sofa. They haven't.
For two months now it's slept like an elephant in the front garden.
Enough is enough. Rain-soaked, it's in the kitchen. We've got the hammer,
saw, kitchen scissors and enough aggression to kick the fucker
to fuckerywoo and as I scissor the hide from the arm, I'm like a nurse
cutting off a cast and we kick and saw all our frustrations. You swing
the hammer; Bang the council: Bang British Gas: Bang the bloody rain:
Bang the boiler and we strip the foam from the frame, you pulling
industrial staples with a screwdriver like a medieval dentist;
un-manufacturing, going through the assembly process backwards,
archaeologists of the recent and in the yard I tug the textile like a hide
or pelt, feeling I'm an Inuit skinning a bear and the carcass and bones
of it sit there.

The sofa's been good to us. Everyday it's been there to comfort us,
sustain us. It deserves a better end than the landfill and having done it
me sen, I'd recommend it as one of those things to do at least once
in your life, smash up your sofa. Our boilers bust, we're nithered and
knackered, so of the sofa, the struts and frame are now all broke wood.
It feels good, oh yeah, we'll have heat tonight. From it's innards, a hair slide,
a crayon, the snapped string of its muscles and tendons, a coin of foreign
denomination, a plastic integral part to a child's game, the coils, the waterfall
of the springs that used to artwork our back, hacked out, the bent tacks,
a good bucket full of ancient fluff and old dust. All into the wheelie bin.
Hull City Council will take it. One way or another they WILL take it.

HULL

It's like that bloke at the bus stop
with a carrier bag full of bacon
going along the queue, *Like bacon?*
Everyone says no. Even I say no.

I love bacon, but I tell a lie
and I admire something about them,
that finds one by my side, here,
8:30 in the morning at the crossing.

Eh mate, do you like whisky?
Yeah, but I got four bottles
for Christmas.
What about Smirnoff?

I tell him, I don't have any money
on me, right at that moment. *Fair enough*,
he shrugs. I don't tell him the truth.
I don't buy stolen goods.

It's one of those things you don't do,
like drinking milk in a pub.

SLUBBERDEGULLION

It's no joke when you're at work
with someone who loves work so much
they can stand and watch it all day,
or should that be, slouch on a broom,
or a roll of carpet would suffice
as a seat or a bed for Potato couch,
a slattern by all accounts, a slowback,
a slacker, a slowpoke, a loafer,
a skrimshanker, a wastrel, a skiver.
If not skiving he's chucking a sickey,
or slumped under the duvet snoozing,
lallygagging, kipping, sleeping in.
His forty winking and work-shy ways
spread like a blood infection
deflating my spizzerinktum
below the level of a zest-less lemon
and I slipped into the slow lane,
oversleeping, jigging, going missing,
bone idle, lackadaisical, too slothful
to concentrate on leaping sheep,
yawning through my sluggardly motions
in slow motion...
Preferring the languid pace of a tortoise
tottering behind a sauntering snail.
I'm a slatternly slugabed, a lacklustre
punch-line. Look me up in the dictionary,
slubberdegullion, boom, boom.

FUNNY BONE

Doctor, doctor, help,
I've got no sense of humour.
The doctor enthuses, let me help you,

knock knock.
Who's there?
Lydia.
Lydia who?
Lydia dustbin just blew off.

See, that's it. I'm sure it's a very funny joke,
but I don't know how to react,
I don't know what laugh to do.
A big belly laugh?
A middle class titter?
A boorish grunter?
Or a polite medium sized, five ha, laugh?
Or whether to just say,
yeah, good one?

"Oh," the doctor goes, "Tell me about your childhood."

So I tell him everything, including
the Sunday my dad got back from the Imperial,
hunted around for his dinner, found a jam pastie
in the oven, took it into' front room,
covered it in gravy.

It was the funniest thing ever,
but his furious temper...
I couldn't laugh. Don't you see.

THE BOISTEROUS SHIRT

Ha ha! Green meanies, Blue Bols, a bottle of Pils
and a bottle of *Merrydown*. Bouncers monitor
your progress, politely remind you of the prohibition
on mixing drinks in *The Golden Fleece*, how you
would be asked to leave the premises should you
flaunt the regulations. So what else can you do?
You mix your meanie, chuck it down your neck,
get kicked out. And you're proud of it! Proud to be ejected
and barred, by a buah, a masculine one, mind,
who looks like she might possibly do Kung Fu.
You roll out into The Stonebow. Destination *Casanova's
Nightclub*, in your boisterous shirt, loudest in town.
Your fabulous shirts holler lewd comments, and are alive,
studded with sequins, stitched with mini lights, that beat
to the sound of Chicago House, they light up whole cities.
These shirts are every colour you can possibly imagine.
Joseph and his *Technicolor* dream-coat? Who are you?
Who are you? They camouflage micro-camcorders
and broadcast on mini screens her watching her on TV,
and always we get them, these lasses in inadvisable
clothing for the time of year, beelining us. We don't need
no chat up lines, we live for our shirts. The next day
you wake up counting beer mat stars. Your shirt
is just there, spreading jubilation through your veins.
You know you haven't wasted your night, your life.

IN THAT DIRECTION

Go past Pound Land, past Everything
For a Pound, by Pound Squeezer,
Pound Finder, Pound Pincher,
Pound Pounder, Pound Squasher,
Pound Basher, Pound Pound Pound;
Make a beeline for It's a Quid;
Turn right at Purveyors of the Finest
Quality Gifts For a Pound; it's
next door to Mighty Pound. If you
reach Pound Fayre, turn round, too far;
Go back to The Quid Squad opposite
Wonder Pound turn right at Planet Pound;
Go on by Poundemonium, One Pound
Please; One Pound Please Sir; One
Pound Please Madame; The Original
Pound Shop, by that one that was there
first, The Pound Zone; up past A Pound
It Is and there you go, there you have it,
there it is, Everything You Need 10p.